New Balance

Matéa Ewen

BookLeaf Publishing

Presentation by *BookLeaf Publishing*

Web: www.bookleafpub.com

E-mail: info@bookleafpub.com

ISBN: 978-93-95784-21-4

First edition 2022

DEDICATION

To everyone who has supported me in pursuing my passion for the art of writing. Especially you, reading this book.

PREFACE

Hello, author speaking here. I'm passionate about poetry, and expressing my ideas and feelings through my words. Like many, I use poetry as a creative outlet to fuel healing from any wounds I may have developed from painful experiences I've had over the years. I wrote these poems with the intention that anyone reading can find safety and solace in my writing style and the poems themselves, just as I have found the same in writing them.

Growth

I remember one day I asked my mother
About those simple wooden slabs
Fixed in the ground next to a baby tree
That felt 10 miles taller than me

She walked me to school
through the soft freshly fallen snow
on that cold winter morning
where our breath turned to ice
and I was bundled tightly with her scarf

I had never seen those slabs before
Where we were from
I only ever saw trees
which circumference seemed
10 times that of my length

To answer my question
She told me they held the trees upright
So they don't fall when the breeze blows too
roughly
Or a bird gets caught in them

It helps them grow

But it never occurred to me how much help we
both needed to grow

We moved soon after.

My First Love

I had my first love at fourteen.
Back then I thought I found it,
but this was when the grass was still green
and I was smitten

For those three months my head was in a cloud
and I was dreaming
I wanted to make him proud
but of that word, I didn't know the meaning.

At a young age, he married.
She's beautiful, like you wouldn't believe
and soon after they bore a legacy—
they conceived.

I used to reminisce
But now
at a time like this
where I walk, on this ground
I couldn't conceive
being with anyone other than me

007

I was wearing my favourite outfit

Those bell bottom pants
With hearts for pockets

And much like my pockets
I wore my heart on my sleeve

Then you gripped me
In places that were not obscene
But made me want to shed my skin

And you ruined my night—
You ruined everything.

You ruined my life.

Reunión

5

You nearly tripped over the shoes
At the front door
When you hugged me
For the first time in forever

And when you hugged me you squeezed
All of your love into me

Your tears stained my neck
And I gripped the back of your shirt
And smiled into you

I still smile thinking of that time

Poltergeist

I seem to leave peoples lives
Dramatically
Or without a trace
As if I were a ghost
Removing my very memory
from the presence of their minds

I don't believe it's healthy
But it's how I've always done things

My emotions curl around my neck
And constrict my breath
Leaving me unable to communicate

My only two options were to explode
Or silently slip away
In an unsuspecting manner

I tell myself that this
is the better option

Female Companionship

With her cool demeanour I almost believed we couldn't be. But now, every time I make her laugh or she sheds tears while confiding in me her deepest fears, or even when her eyes brighten with the beams of a thousand stars when excited, time stops.

And I realize just how grateful I am…

To be a friend of hers.

Artificial Intelligence

I feel as though I simply mirror
the expressions,
mannerisms,
and emotions of others
As feeling and acting in my own right
seem to be inherently wrong

Collecting data before I engage
Is merely how I learned to operate

Analyzing
Correcting
Executing
Is my process

Trying to rewrite my program feels impossible
During this new phase in my life
The database must be scrubbed
New data must be absorbed
But this process takes time

My motherboard feels damaged
But it came this way

And in the meantime I feel as lost
As an android discarded

Sick Sad World

Reading the news makes the inner mechanisms
of my digestive system twist and turn

If only I could crush the earth beneath my feet in
order to remedy the human condition

I often contemplate the reason for our existence,
if there even is one

Where was the end we were promised?
Instead we keep looping, as if we're perpetually
stuck on this merry go round

The earth spins and so do we.

Oscillating Fan

It seemed like each year that passed
I learned just how many differences
We actually had

Not that this was a driving force
Or factor
In the natural process of separation

But it was evidence of growth
It was evidence of seek and find
It was evidence of finding ourselves
Outside of each other

But for some reason his preference
Of an oscillating fan
And mine for stillness
Plays on my mind like a record
I have trouble stopping

But I'd never scratch in a million years

Insufficient Funds

One, two, three coins
you placed in the machine
Moving that joystick ever so slightly
Your eyes narrowed on the prize

It took forever
Before you pressed that big red button
Making that claw descend
And you were determined

But the prize slipped out of your grasp
Once again
You cursed to yourself
And reached into your pocket

To fish out some more coins
To win that beloved prize

But they were empty

That was your last chance
And you hadn't even realized it

Upon a Star

I wish I could turn back time
And be fully transparent

I wish I didn't just vanish
I was in a trance like state

Blinded by a new feeling of liberation

We both know we felt trapped
But in two different ways
On two opposite sides

I wish I was able to tell you
How much it hurt to be in contact with you
I felt like I'd be hurting you too much
By even letting these words escape my lips

Ironically
It probably hurt even more
That I just left
Without a single trace

And you came back wanting to reconcile
But I was scorned by your cruel words
Although said a while back

Bitterness stained me
Somehow I felt you should've known
I felt that because you held a special place
In my mind
And in my heart
you would know what I was thinking
And how I was feeling
Automatically

I was wrong to assume.
We were wrong about a lot of things.
I know neither of us expected to be here

But here we are

And all I can do is wish

Wish upon a star

Esoteric

Some people find solace
In the God they were introduced to
In their youth

Some people find solace
In the abandonment of it

In the same way mental cleansing
Isn't the same as brainwashing

So are spirituality and religion
Respectively.

Buoyancy

Clear blue waves
crash against the top of my feet
and my toes stay buried
beneath the sand soaked with it

The salted cool breeze
brushes past the skin on my cheeks
and brings me back to reality

For a moment
and just a moment
I almost forgot what it felt like

to be alive

Abyss

My breath couldn't catch up
To legs that refused to slow
My side began aching
And sweat dripped past my brow

But I kept on

I turned it into a game
Like patty cake
Or better yet— manhunt
To see how far I could get
Away from the abyss
Before it caught up with me
And swallowed me whole

Again.

Reaching further and further
Than the last time

Each time

It was a never ending cycle
It's all I can remember
All I can think of

It consumes the mind
It consumes the body

I think the abyss is gone
But I'm not sure
I still don't look back
Lest I turn to a pillar of salt

Everyone is telling me the abyss is gone
Even my brain tells me

But my body won't stop
It can't stop

Because the last time it caught up to me

I almost couldn't find my way out

And I refuse to let it happen again

Communion

We sit in those familiar pews
Awaiting the sermon
Our daily bread

We inject this feeling
Of euphoria
Into our veins
Hoping that it will last
Till the end of the week
When we return to these pews
And we can get our next fix

But it's always fleeting
Because we go back
To living our same lives
Hurting the same people
Including ourselves
Repeatedly
Until we return to the sanctuary

Our supposed safe haven

Only to do the same thing
Again
And again

Until we reach our inevitable end

Pearly Whites

I've always had a thing
for men with pretty hands
And smiles that could take your breath away

And yet
What I'd always expect
Was for them to breathe life into me

But they couldn't
And they never would

Because those smiles
Those beautiful pearly whites
We're only capable of taking

They would never be able to provide

Plinian Eruption

The conversation we had before last
Felt like a stifled cry under my duvet
I believed I was moving on fast
But I was a crack in a dam ready to burst
And my emotions were too hard to convey

I realized I took for granted you putting me first

The pot bubbled over
And I was left with a curse

Ruby Red

Red used to be my favourite
Red velvet cake
Red rain-boots
Big red bows and bright red shoes
Sunsets kissed by shades of red

And normally I charge towards the sight of red.
Like a bull provoked.

But maybe I had a rose coloured view of red
Maybe I forced myself to tolerate her
Because she was inescapable
Red ink, of which I was forbidden to use
tainting my best work in class—
patronizing me, judging me, failing me.
Red alarms invoking anxiety.
Red flags in men.
The blood I coughed up in the morning..
The same blood that would leak onto the bed—
that painted my sheets.
I was mourning.

The gas light, again.

But I was impartial

because I claimed her my friend.

I should've acknowledged and appreciated the
duality of red
As she was both a symbol of comfort and a
signal of danger.

I was powerless against red.
She threatened and dominated me.
I didn't know any other way of life
other than being subdued by her

So this time I charge in the opposite direction of
red
I want nothing to do with it
I know now
that nothing good comes of it

I've learned my crimson lesson

Knock Knock Joke

Knock knock
Who's there?
Death

When death knocks at the door
The questions you have
Will always go unanswered

Sometimes death, he doesn't knock
Sometimes he barges right in
And your house of cards will collapse
with you in it

All you can do
is find it in your heart to accept him.
One cannot ignore death away
like one does with the Jehovah's Witnesses
who claim to bring life
to those that answer

Pitying
Or deterring him
by paying him off
as if he was a Girl Scout
Selling sickly sweet cookies

Will only send him away
but for only a moment

Sadly
he always returns

And one cannot know the hour
Nor the day

Death knocks as but a warning
He knocks
and knocks
but it's easier for us to laugh
to the rhythm of it

As if it were a knock knock joke.

A knock knock joke, lacking in humor.

Russian Doll

Each layer of me
Feels like a shell
Of the girl I once knew

Each life event that passes
A new shell hardens around me as if I were
a Russian doll waiting to be broken
To reveal the me within it

With a Tootsie Pop, the question has always
been
How long it will take to get to the centre of it
With my Russian doll
The question will always be
How long it will take to forget the centre of it

Cardiovascular Defect

I was born with a hole in my heart
Which grew three times its size
And nearly tore itself apart

The hole held a specific shape
A particular form
Unfamiliar to most
Of which nothing could fill

I spent so long
Nearly half my life
Attempting to find the piece
That could fit into that small
Yet never ending hole

I stopped at nothing
Thinking that someone or something
Outside of me could complete it

I didn't realize
That I had the missing piece
To fill it all along